Red around you

Shirley Page

This book tells you about the colour red, where it comes from and what makes it special as a colour. It helps you notice the many different ways red is used around us every day.

If you are using the book to find out particular facts about red around you, you do not have to read it all. Look in the **contents** (below) or the **index** (at the back) to find the best pages to help you. Then just read as much as you need to read.

The basic facts are given in big print, and more detailed information is in smaller print. You can find details about the paintings used in this book on page 24.

Contents

1	The qualities of red	2
2	Natural red	4
3	Chemical red	6
4	Red pigment	8
5	Red in light	10
6	Why red is bright	12
7	How we see red	14
8	How red affects other colours	16
9	Who uses red?	18
10	Where we see red	20
11	Red in festivals	22
	Glossary	23
	Further information	24
	Index	25

1 The qualities of red

True red is called brilliant red. It is the strongest pure red colour. Other shades of red have little bits of other colours in them.

All the groups of reds have different names so that we can tell them apart and describe them accurately. Most reds are warm colours. They make us think of sunsets, warm fires, glowing embers, and heat. Red is a comforting, warming colour, and it makes us feel good.

↑ Shades of red

Groups of reds have distinctive names and different qualities.
Orange reds are called vermilion, cadmium red and scarlet. They are brilliant and fiery. Pink reds include rose madder and cerise which are soft and gentle. Blue reds are called crimson and carmine. They are rich and glowing. Brownish reds are earth and brick colours. They are called terracotta, venetian red and red iron oxide.

Looking at red makes you feel warm.

2 Natural red

Long ago, people could only make colours from the natural substances available to them. Natural reds were made from coloured earths and clays, from the roots of plants, and from some insects.

⬆ Cave paintings showing bison and mammoths painted in red.

About 15,000 to 10,000 years BC, cave dwellers were some of the first people to use red clay and earth to make paints for their pictures. They painted bison and mammoths on their cave walls. Much later, around 3000 BC, people discovered other ways of making red. They found that the root of the madder plant could be used to make red. At about the same time, people living in Peru and people in the Canary Islands discovered how to make red dye from crushing beetles.

Natural dyes and paints

Red clay is a kind of soil with iron in it and it produces a strong brick red colour. It can be used to colour pottery and to make a paint. Natural reds are also made from the roots of madder plants.

Madder is a herb. It is a small plant with delicate yellow flowers. The roots of the plant contain red juices that can be taken out by boiling the roots and collecting the liquid. This makes a strong red dye.

Some insects can also make natural red. Cochineal is a scarlet dye made from the dried husks of coccus beetles, which live on cactus plants in Mexico, Peru and the Caribbean islands. Cochineal is still used for food colouring today.

⬆ Coccus beetles on a cactus plant

⬆ Madder. This small herb is one of only a few plants that will make a crimson red dye.

3 Chemical red

Natural reds were used until about 1600 AD. At that time, scientists began to find new ways of making reds. They experimented with a wide variety of the new materials that were being discovered. More recently, chemists have found ways of making reds from metals, coal and oil.

As people learnt more about chemistry in the eighteenth and nineteenth centuries, they discovered ways of making reds from metals like cadmium.

In the last 40 or 50 years, chemists have found many more ways of making reds out of chemicals. Scientists have created red dyes from coal-tar and oil. The dyes made from coal tar are called Azo dyes. Some of these are used today to make some of our foods red.

Azo dyes are manufactured in laboratories. Scientists can make millions of different shades of red.

⬆ You often eat and drink chemical reds.

Synthetic dyes

The most recent dyes made from chemicals, coal-tar and oil are called synthetic dyes. They are artificial – that is, not made from substances we find in nature. These new dyes are stronger than natural ones. This means that brighter shades of red can be made in order to colour plastics, fabrics and paint.

Red colours are added to some foods and drinks. One of the most frequently used is a red **E** number dye called E122 carmoisine or azo rubine. Look on the labels of food packets and tins. You will find E122 in tinned fruit, in packets of jelly and in soft drinks, especially cherryade.

4 Red pigment

Red pigment is the earth or dye from which crayons and paints are made. The pigment is made into a fine powder and mixed with glue and chalk to make crayons, or it is mixed with oil to make paints. It can be made from both natural and chemical reds.

Pigments were first made by cave men who used red earth, mixed with water, as a paint. More ways of making red were discovered. Pigments were used to make different sorts of paints and crayons.

Pigment was mixed with glue to make crayons and pastels. To make water-colour blocks, gum arabic and glycerine were added to pigment. To make oil paints, oils from plants like linseed and poppy were mixed with pigment.

You can also get red pigment as a powder. All you have to do is add water to make a liquid paint. Pigment can be bought in various shades of red and other colours.

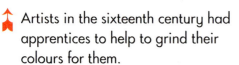

Artists in the sixteenth century had apprentices to help to grind their colours for them.

■ Nowadays pigment is made by the firms who supply schools and artists with the colours they need. When you use red powder colour, you add your own water to the pigment to make it liquid. You can paint it on to paper with a brush. There is a choice of several different red pigments already in powder form.

■ In the past artists used to have to grind their own powder from solid blocks of red earth, stones and metals. They had to make it into paint by adding egg or different sorts of oils. Artists now use ready made oil paints which have been made by manufacturers.

■ There are many different shades of red which can be bought. They have many unusual names to describe exact shades of red so that the artist will know which one to choose for a particular effect.

⬆ Today's artists use ready-made reds.

⬆ Oil paints: Light Red, Alizarin Crimson, Cadmium Red Hue, Scarlet Lake.

5 Red in light

All natural light on earth comes from the sun. It is the star at the centre of our solar system.

⬆ The sun appears bigger at sunset.

The sun is very important in our solar system. It is made up of hot gases, and it gives off heat and light to the planets. Earth is one of the planets. (There are other suns or stars in other solar systems).

Light wavelengths

Light contains all the colours there are, and we can prove this when we see the colours in rainbows and sunsets. Our light travels through space in wavelengths in a similar way to waves moving across the sea. In the wavelengths of light, red is the longest and strongest colour.

The colours in the sun's light can be seen most clearly at dawn and at dusk, as the light is getting stronger at dawn, or as it is fading away at dusk.

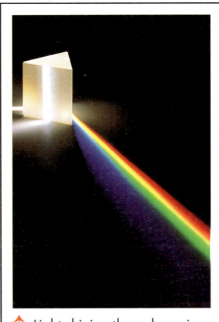

Light shining through a prism.

Some people believe a rainbow is a promise that things will get better.

6 Why red is bright

Light and colour travel through space in waves. Each colour has a different wavelength. Red has the longest wavelength.

Red has the longest wavelength and is also the strongest colour because it reflects more light than other colours.

Red inks or paints show up against other colours. They look nearer and clearer.

Red stands out. It brings the other colours to life. Cover the reds with pieces of pale green paper and see how dull the painting looks.

Activity 1: Proving that red looks bigger

Materials you need
- Brightly coloured pieces of paper in red, blue and green. (Shiny paper is best, like that used in Sunday newspaper colour supplements).
- White paper for a background to stick the coloured pieces on.
- Glue.

Follow this process

1 Cut out squares of the same size in red, blue and green. Some should be 5 cm squares and some 2 cm squares.

2 Stick one small red square in the centre of a large blue square.

3 Stick another small red square in the centre of a larger green square.

4 Stick a small blue square on a larger square of red.

5 Stick a small green square on a larger square of red.

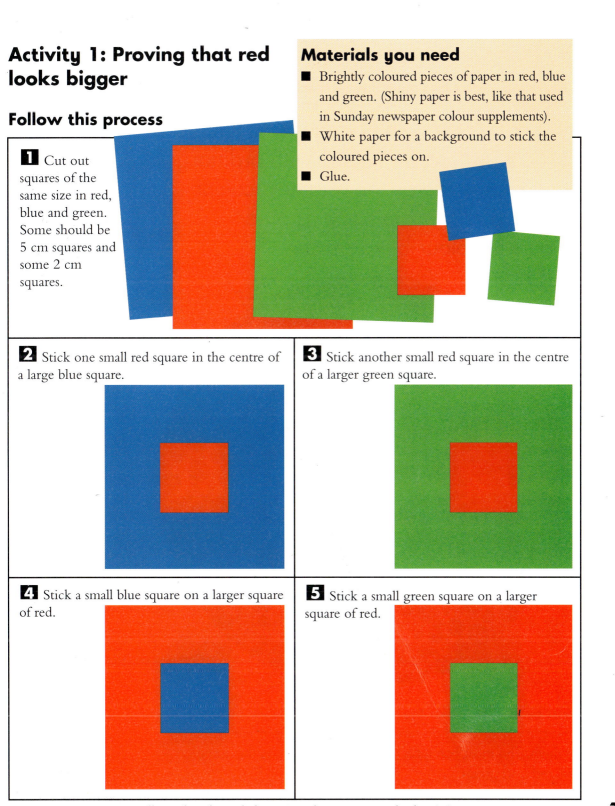

You will see that the red always stands out more, whether it is on top or underneath. This is because red is the strongest colour. It is what we call the dominant colour.

7 How we see red

We see colours with our eyes and with parts of our brains. People with ordinary eyesight see red as the brightest colour. But red can look the same as other colours to colour-blind people.

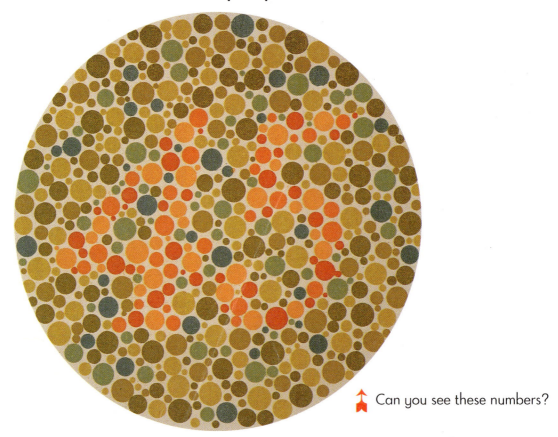

⬆ Can you see these numbers?

Most people see red as the strongest colour. Many people who are colour blind do not. Red can seem like other colours to them. The most common colours to be seen as the same are red and green.

Colour blindness runs in families and it almost always affects the men rather than the women. It does not alter the way people see.

Living with colour blindness

Colour blindness makes no difference to most of the people who are colour blind. They quickly learn that signs and signals have positions and patterns as well as colour. For example, traffic lights do not rely just on colours. Red is always at the top and green is always at the bottom. Other red lights flash, and red flags wave, to attract attention.

The people who are most affected by colour blindness are those who would like to be pilots. Colour-blind people cannot fly planes. Other jobs which are not open to colour-blind people include some in the policeforce, the fire service, and the Post Office. Some jobs on the railways cannot be done by colour-blind people.

Artists are sometimes colour blind. They paint the colours they see and sometimes this makes a painting more interesting.

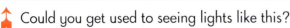
Could you get used to seeing lights like this?

8 How red affects other colours

Pure red is the warmest colour. When it is added to other colours, it makes them look brighter or darker. When red is mixed with yellow, it makes the yellow look warmer. When it is added to blue, the colour looks cooler.

When red is mixed with yellow, it is still a warm colour. We use it for painting sunlight and the flames in a fire. Red mixed with pale blue makes a soft lilac purple which is often used for painting shadows. Red mixed with yellow and blue makes a whole range of warm and cool browns which can be used for bricks, wood, and earth.

Red looks closer than other colours

Red looks closer than other colours. In paintings or coloured pictures, the red will always stand out more. If you want to use red in paintings, you need to know how to stop it looking too bright. When painting you can add small amounts of other colours to take away some of the red's brightness.

Green is a cool colour and looks further away than red in a painting. To make a painting of a landscape with red poppies in it, add a tiny bit of green paint to the red paint. It will soften the red so that it looks the same distance away as the green. An artist called Claude Monet made some paintings of poppies which show this effect.

Activity 2 Softening colours

Materials you need
- Water colours or powder paints.
- Firm white paper.
- Paint brush.
- Water.

Follow this process

1 Paint a picture using warm, glowing colours such as orange, red, pink and brownish reds, as in the painting of poppies.

2 Now paint a picture of the same or a similar subject, but using pale red, crimson, bluish pinks, grey-blues and greens.

3 Compare the two pictures and see how very different they make you feel.

⬆ The poppies are painted in warm colours. The other painting looks much cooler.

9 Who uses red?

Artists often use red in their pictures. Sometimes only a tiny brushful of red is used, but this one bit of red brings the rest of the painting to life.

There were two famous artists who used red in their work.

John Constable lived and worked in Suffolk. He painted many landscapes. In most of them, he used a touch of red to contrast with all the different shades of green.

Graham Sutherland was born in London but he spent a lot of time painting scenes in Pembrokeshire. He used his imagination to remember the places he had seen.

Landscape pictures, like the one by John Constable, show real scenes of trees and fields. They are usually made up of lots of different shades of green. To bring some contrast to all the greenness, all landscape artists almost always use a touch of red.

John Constable made many paintings of Salisbury Cathedral. You can see his paintings in the Tate Gallery and other galleries in London.

Colour wheel

Look at the colour wheel in the picture. Red is opposite green. This means that green is the 'complementary' colour to red. It is the most different from red, and so it gives the maximum contrast. Colours on opposite sides of the colour wheel bring each other to life.

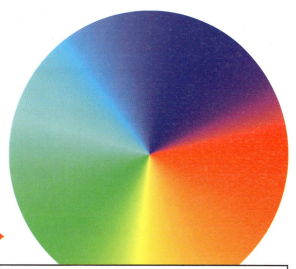

Red and green are complementary colours. ➡

⬆ Graham Sutherland is a famous artist. He has a whole art gallery devoted to his work. It is the Graham Sutherland Gallery at The Rhos, Dyfed, Wales.

In *Red Landscape*, Graham Sutherland has used red to show us how a landscape might look in special circumstances. These could be unusual weather conditions or different times of day. He may have wanted us to see how empty and deserted this land is. Although he has used a cheerful colour, he has managed here to make it look sombre and dark.

10 Where we see red

Lots of people use red because it is bright and it attracts our attention. Red is used by advertisers and by the emergency services like the fire brigade. It is also used for messages and notices.

Red catches the eye.

Red is used by the Post Office, by advertisers and by the emergency services. They use red because of its brightness and because we see red as being important. Red is often used in school. The teachers use a red pencils or pens to correct work or to give marks for good work.

⬆ The Post Office started using red for their vans as long ago as 1938.

We see red around us every day. The Post Office uses red for its letter boxes, delivery vans, shop signs, and Parcel Force uses red because red is so easily seen.

Advertisers use red because they want to persuade us to buy their goods. Red on labels and packets makes us want to choose those items first.

The emergency services like fire engines and the Red Cross use red so that they can immediately be seen and recognised.

11 Red in festivals

Red is a bright and joyful colour, so it is used in festivals. It is also used for decorations and clothing. Festivals are happy celebrations and all countries have them.

There are many festivals around the world that use red. Festivals are happy days or occasions where everybody is celebrating. Often feasts or good food are part of the festival.

▲ A Tilak is made from red powder.

When people celebrate Christmas, many traditional things are red. Houses are decorated with holly which is enjoyed for its shiny red berries and people buy red plants such as poinsettias. Christmas is a Christian festival.

Divali is the festival of light. It is celebrated by Hindu people. They light lamps in honour of their God Rama. Another important ceremony at Divali is called Puja when people close old account books and open new ones to mark a new financial year. For this ceremony they wear a Tilak, which is a red mark on the forehead.

Glossary of words used in this book

Advertiser — An advertiser is someone who writes or makes up advertisements to persuade people to buy certain products.

Bison — A bison is a large, quiet, grass-eating animal which was hunted by people for food.

Chemistry — Chemistry is one of part of science. It looks at how things are made and how they change.

Colour wheel — A colour wheel is a way of arranging the colours so that they form a circle. One half has warm colours, the other half has cool colours. Complementary colours are opposite each other, across the circle.

Coal tar — Coal tar is a thick black liquid. When coal is heated to make gas for cooking and heating, coal tar is left behind.

Dawn — Dawn is when the sun rises. It is the start of a new day.

Divali — Divali is a happy Hindu festival. Lots of lamps are lit so there is lots of light.

Dominant — A dominant colour is more important than other colours, it is more noticeable.

Dusk — Dusk is when the sun sinks down below the horizon. It is the end of the day.

Hindu — A Hindu is a person who believes in one of the religions that is common in India and other countries.

Horizon — A horizon is the line at where the land or sea seems to meet the sky.

Laboratory — A laboratory is a place where scientific work is carried out, a place for finding things out.

Landscape — A landscape is a view or a picture of part of the countryside taken from one place.

Mammoth — A mammoth was a large, fierce hairy creature, similar to an elephant. Mammoths are now extinct.

Pigment — Pigment is a fine dry power or dye which gives paint its colour.

Prism — A prism is a triangular piece of glass which separates light into its individual colours.

Tone — Tone is a word that describes whether a colour is light or dark.

Further information

The best way to find out more about red is to look for it and see how often it is used.

Red appears in lots of paintings. Visit your local art and craft shop and look for pictures with red in them. You may be able to buy postcards of some of them to take home and study to find out more about them.

Many Museums and Art Galleries now have an Education Officer who will help you about the paintings and the artists.

Further reading

Just Look by Robert Cumming, Kestrel Books 1979

The Colour Eye by Robert Cumming and Tom Porter, BBC 1990

Have a good look with Johnny Morris by Johnny Morris, Dobson 1979

Enjoying Pictures by Helen Knapp, Routledge, Kegan and Paul 1975

Picture this by Felicity Way, Hodder and Stoughton 1989

More than meets the eye: a closer look at paintings in the National Gallery by M. Cassin, National Gallery 1987

Paintings used in this book

Page 3	*By the fireside* by Joseph Oppenheimer, Christie's London
Page 4	*Bisons from the caves at Altamira* by an unknown artist, Altamira, Spain
Page 11	*The blind girl* by Sir John Everett Milas, Birmingham City Museums and Art Gallery
Page 12	*The bathers, Dieppe* by Walter Sickert, Walker Art Gallery, Liverpool
Page 17	*Poppies* by Fiona Fleming, Private Collection
Page 17	*Vermilion and mauve* by Winifred Nicholson, Christie's London
Page 18	*Salisbury Cathedral from the meadows* by John Constable, Private Collection
page 19	*Red landscape* by Graham Sutherland, Southampton Art Gallery
page 21	*Loading mail at Euston Station* by Grace Golden, Royal Mail Collection.